SPOTLIGHT ON GEORGIA

DEVELOPMENTS IN GEORGIA AFTER WORLD WAR II

SAM CROMPTON

PowerKiDS press.

NEW YORK

Published in 2018 by The Rosen Publishing Group, Inc.
29 East 21st Street, New York, NY 10010

Editor: Melissa Raé Shofner
Book Design: Michael Flynn

Photo Credits: Cover Howell Walker/National Geographic/Getty Images; p. 5 SuperStock/Getty Images; pp. 6, 9, 11, 12, 13 Bettmann/Getty Images; p. 7 Myron Davis/The LIFE Picture Collection/Getty Images; pp. 14, 15 Courtesy of Library of Congress; p. 17 Grey Villet/The LIFE Picture Collection/Getty Images; p. 19 (main) Thomas Barrat/Shutterstock.com; p. 19 (inset) EQRoy/Shutterstock.com; p. 21 ESB Professional/ Shutterstock.com; p. 23 Joe Holloway Jr./AP Images; p. 25 AP Images; p. 26 Collegiate Images/Getty Images; p. 27 Focus On Sport/Getty Images; p. 29 Tony Evans/Timelapse Library Ltd./Hulton Archive/Getty Images.

Cataloging-in-Publication Data

Names: Crompton, Sam.
Title: Developments in Georgia after World War II / Sam Crompton.
Description: New York : PowerKids Press, 2018. | Series: Spotlight on Georgia | Includes index.
Identifiers: ISBN 9781508160212 (pbk.) | ISBN 9781508160243 (library bound) | ISBN 9781508160229 (6 pack)
Subjects: LCSH: Georgia--Juvenile literature. | World War, 1939-1945--Juvenile literature.
Classification: LCC F286.3 C76 2018 | DDC 975.8--dc23

Manufactured in the United States of America

CPSIA Compliance Information: Batch #BS17PK For further information contact Rosen Publishing, New York, New York at 1-800-237-9932.

CONTENTS

CHAPTER ONE

CHANGING TIMES

World War II changed the lives of many people in Georgia. After the war ended in 1945, Georgians disagreed about what direction the state should head in. Some wished for social and racial relations to remain the same. Others wished to change them. Some Georgians were eager to see industry grow and become more important. Others wished for the farming way of life to be preserved.

Right after World War II, Georgia experienced an unusual political situation. Three men claimed the position of governor at the same time. This event left its mark on Georgians. Where politics were concerned, they likely felt less secure than their parents and grandparents felt.

For those who wanted a return to the good old days, nothing seemed more appealing than sports and entertainment. These are two industries that became more important after World War II.

World War II brought about many changes in Georgia. It lead to rising urbanization, or the growth of cities, and many changes in race relations.

CHAPTER TWO

GOVERNOR ARNALL

Ellis Arnall was a native Georgian who moved up in life rather quickly. Arnall was born in Newnan, Georgia, in 1907. He entered the state **legislature** at the young age of 25. He became attorney general of Georgia at 31. In 1942, he defeated Eugene Talmadge in the race for governor. He was 35 years old, which made him the youngest governor in the country at the time.

Eugene Talmadge served three terms as Georgia's governor between 1933 and 1943.

Ellis Arnall served as the governor of Georgia from 1943 until 1947.

This was no small feat. Talmadge had practically owned the governorship for nearly a decade. Arnall took over as Georgia's wartime governor. He worked closely with President Franklin D. Roosevelt. The federal government provided Georgia with funding for military installations and defense contracts during Arnall's time in office.

As World War II came to a close, Arnall had many reasons to be proud of his accomplishments. He had steered the Peach State through a period of great **crisis**.

CHAPTER THREE

THE END OF THE WHITE PRIMARIES

Ellis Arnall was a person ahead of his time. He worked to improve the voting rights of black citizens. Many white Georgians did not share his vision, however.

In *King v. Chapman* in 1945, a federal court struck down the all-white **primary** system for the Democratic Party in Georgia. This system kept blacks from voting in the Democratic Party primaries. At this time in Georgia, the person who won the Democratic nomination was almost certain to win the statewide election. After the *King v. Chapman* ruling, this political security for whites in Georgia was removed. Arnall didn't fight this ruling, which angered many white Georgians. Eugene Talmadge, however, fought against *King v. Chapman* as part of his campaign platform in 1946.

In another twist, a new amendment, or change, to Georgia's state constitution declared that no governor could **succeed** himself in office. Arnall, therefore, could not run for reelection in 1946.

During his time as governor, Arnall reworked Georgia's state constitution and paid off $36 million owed by the state.

CHAPTER FOUR

THREE GOVERNORS OF GEORGIA

In 1946, Eugene Talmadge made a remarkable political comeback. He ran in and won the Democratic primary that year. He also won the 1946 fall election. Eugene Talmadge was about to begin his fourth term as Georgia's governor when he died.

After Talmadge's death, Melvin E. Thompson, who had been chosen as lieutenant governor in the election, claimed the position of governor. So did Herman Talmadge, Eugene's son. To make things even more confusing, Arnall said he wouldn't give up the office of governor until the situation was clear.

In January 1947, the Georgia General Assembly elected Herman Talmadge governor. Thompson took his case to the Georgia Supreme Court, which made him the acting governor in March 1947. However, in September 1948, Herman Talmadge was elected governor in a special election. Talmadge served the final two years of the term.

While in office, Herman E. Talmadge, pictured here, supported the separation of racial groups.

CHAPTER FIVE

AFRICAN AMERICANS AT THE POLLS

Despite the political turmoil in Georgia, 1946 was a breakthrough election year. The previous year, in the *King v. Chapman* case, a federal court ruled the whites-only primary was unconstitutional. African Americans couldn't be excluded, or left out, of the primaries as they were a vital part of the election process.

This photo, which was taken in 1946, shows African Americans preparing to vote.

Thousands of African Americans in Marietta, Georgia, showed up to vote in the Democratic primaries in July 1946.

African Americans were now able to register to vote and participate in the Democratic primary. Even so, many people doubted whether blacks would turn out to vote. To encourage them not to, **white supremacists** placed signs with hostile messages at polling booths and post offices.

Despite warnings of violence, African Americans refused to back down. The Atlanta Urban League and other groups worked to organize voters in 1946. Together, these groups were able to register more than 14,000 new African American voters in just two months.

CHAPTER SIX

CHANGES ON THE FARM

Georgia continued to be a big agricultural producer after World War II. However, the way crops were planted and harvested was changing. Tractors first appeared in the 1930s and became more popular during the 1940s. The first mechanical cotton pickers arrived in the late 1940s. These new machines could be operated by one person and do work that was once done by many. They could also cover larger amounts of land in much less time.

This photo shows a young boy plowing a cotton field in Valdosta, Georgia, in 1915.

Cotton-picking machines could harvest cotton faster than people could. This one could harvest two rows of cotton at once.

With the ability to do more work faster, farms around the state started producing more crops. Better seeds, fertilizers, and pest-control methods were developed. Many farms were able to grow more crops per acre, and some farms grew larger.

Changes in agriculture after World War II left some farm workers without jobs. Many **tenant farmers** and other farm workers moved to cities to seek work in new industrial plants.

CHAPTER SEVEN

WILLIAM B. HARTSFIELD

William B. Hartsfield was born in 1890 and spent his whole life and career in Atlanta. Hartsfield studied law and opened his own law firm in 1921. In 1922, he was elected to the Atlanta City Council. Hartsfield ran for mayor in 1936 and defeated James L. Key, the current mayor.

As mayor, Hartsfield pushed for a policy to save Atlanta money. He thought the city shouldn't spend more than 95 percent of what it had received in taxes the previous year. This new policy allowed Atlanta to flourish more than ever before.

Hartsfield wasn't reelected in 1940. However, the man who beat him that year later resigned his job in order to join the U.S. Army during World War II. Hartsfield won a special election in 1942, and he remained in the mayor's office until 1961. Under Hartfield's guidance, Atlanta **desegregated** its public schools without issue in 1961.

William B. Hartsfield served as the mayor of Atlanta for nearly six terms. This is longer than anyone else in the city's history.

CHAPTER EIGHT

GROWING ATLANTA

During Hartsfield's political career, Atlanta gained a reputation for being friendly to **aviators**. Before he was elected mayor, Hartsfield played an important role in creating the first Atlanta airport. Today, the Hartsfield-Jackson Atlanta International Airport is named partly in his honor.

Mayor Hartsfield wanted people outside Atlanta, especially those from the North, to want to come to his city. Promoting aviation was part of his plan. Hartsfield also worked with Robert W. Woodruff, president of Coca-Cola. Between the two of them, Hartsfield and Woodruff persuaded many workers to move to Atlanta.

The end of World War II signaled a new time for Atlanta. The city population grew dramatically during the late 1940s and early 1950s. Companies such as Ford and General Motors opened new factories near Atlanta, creating many new jobs. Nearly 1,200 national companies had offices in Atlanta by 1954.

The Atlanta City Council renamed the city's airport in honor of Hartsfield a week after his death in 1971.

CHAPTER NINE

HARTSFIELD'S VISION

Mayor Hartsfield had a **profound** vision for Atlanta. Unlike Chicago, Detroit, and many other northern cities, Atlanta had room to expand in all directions. No major river or lake stood in the way. Mayor Hartsfield, therefore, imagined a time when Atlanta would have a better and busier downtown area, complete with skyscrapers. **Suburbs** would surround the downtown area.

In 1951, Hartsfield was elected vice president of the American Municipal Association (AMA). He would eventually become the organization's president. During his time with the AMA, Atlanta tripled in size and its population grew by an estimated 100,000 people.

In June 1961, Hartsfield announced that he wouldn't seek a seventh term as mayor. However, he remained active in politics and the Atlanta community and was named mayor **emeritus**. After his time as mayor, Hartsfield worked as a consultant for several Georgia companies, including Coca-Cola.

In 1952, the city added 82 square miles (212.4 square km) of land and began building major roadways to encourage further growth. Today, downtown Atlanta features skyscrapers and highways.

CHAPTER TEN

MAYOR ALLEN

Ivan Allen Jr. was born in Atlanta in 1911. He was the son of an important businessman. Allen became the mayor of Atlanta in 1962. This was an interesting change, as many younger people in Atlanta couldn't remember a time when William B. Hartsfield had not been their mayor.

Allen played an important role in desegregating Atlanta during the 1960s. On his first day in office, he had all the "colored" and "white" signs removed from city hall. He also desegregated city hall's cafeteria. He worked closely with Martin Luther King Jr.

Allen was the only elected official in the South to go before Congress in support of the bill that would later become the Civil Rights Act of 1964. Even before the law passed, Allen worked closely with the people of Atlanta to desegregate many businesses and public facilities.

In 1981, Ivan Allen Jr. was awarded the Martin Luther King Jr. Nonviolent Peace Prize for his work in race relations in Atlanta. In this photograph from 1969, Allen stands with Coretta Scott King, the widow of Martin Luther King Jr.

CHAPTER ELEVEN

POPULATION GROWTH

The early 20th century had not been kind to Georgia. The 1920s saw many people leave the state. The trend reversed just a decade or so later, however. During the 1930s, Georgia's population grew by 7.4 percent. From the 1940s to the 1950s, the state's population increased by 10.3 percent. Many people moved from rural areas to the cities. All these new people needed many things, including new schools.

As recently as the early 1900s, few Georgians graduated from high school. During the 1950s, however, a high school degree became a badge of honor, as well as a ticket to a job. Young Georgians flocked to the new high schools, which were built in the 1950s and 1960s. Many of these new schools contained up-to-date classrooms, some designed for education in the sciences.

Charlayne Hunter and Hamilton Holmes were the first African American students allowed to attend the University of Georgia. They received their diplomas in 1963.

CHAPTER TWELVE

SPORTS IN GEORGIA

Georgia has become known for the strength of its college sports teams, especially football. The University of Georgia, located in Athens, has one of the oldest college football teams in the country.

At first, Georgia was not considered an ideal place for professional sports teams because it was located far from the national **news media** centers. Cities such as Boston, New York, and Baltimore got professional teams first. Eventually, Georgia was able to join in. In 1966, the Atlanta Falcons played

In 1946, the University of Georgia Bulldogs finished their football season with a perfect record. They also won the national championship game and the Sugar Bowl that year.

Hank Aaron was an outfielder who played for the Atlanta Braves from 1954 to 1974.

their first game. Sadly, few Georgia college players went to the Falcons. In the early years, the team didn't have the money to bring in the best players.

The Braves are a baseball team first located in Boston and later Milwaukee. The team moved south to Atlanta in 1966 and has played its home games there ever since.

CHAPTER THIRTEEN

MUSIC AND FILM

The 1950s and 1960s were very good for Georgia as far as the entertainment industry was concerned. Many moviegoers became more familiar with the Peach State. This was thanks to films—such as *The Great Locomotive Chase*—that were either filmed in Georgia or had Georgia themes.

Two of the most famous Georgia-born musicians of this time were Otis Redding and Ray Charles. Redding was born in Dawson in 1941 and became one of the finest performers of the 1960s. Today, his song "(Sittin' on) The Dock of the Bay" is considered a classic.

Ray Charles was born in Albany, Georgia, in 1930. Blind from the age of seven, Charles became one of the greatest performers of the 20th century. He recorded the song "Georgia on My Mind" in 1960, and it became one of the great popular songs of the decade.

Ray Charles's performance of the song "Georgia on My Mind" was a huge hit and permanently linked his career with his home state.

CHAPTER FOURTEEN

MOVING FORWARD

After World War II ended in 1945, Georgia underwent many changes. The state faced several political problems soon after the war's end. However, there were also many advancements during this time.

New machinery changed the face of agriculture, making it easier and faster to plant and harvest crops. These advancements, coupled with the growth of other industries, caused a population shift from rural areas to cities. Cities grew quickly throughout Georgia. Atlanta led the way, but Savannah, Athens, Albany, and Macon were not far behind.

What was most lacking in Georgia was racial harmony. Much of Georgia was still divided along racial lines. Some people supported equal rights, but others did not. Moving further into the second half of the 20th century, racial **tensions** would come to a head and the civil rights movement would begin.

GLOSSARY

aviator (AY-vee-ay-tuhr) Someone who pilots an airplane.

crisis (KRY-sus) An unstable or difficult situation.

desegregate (dee-SEH-gruh-gayt) To do away with segregation, or the separation of people based on race, class, or ethnicity.

emeritus (eh-MER-uh-tuhs) Holding an honorary title given after retirement.

legislature (LEH-jush-lay-chur) A body of people that has the power to make or pass laws.

news media (NOOS MEE-dee-uh) Sources and presentation of news and information, such as TV, radio, newspapers, magazines, and Internet articles.

primary (PRY-mehr-ee) An election in which members of the same political party run against each other for the chance to be in a larger and more important election.

profound (pruh-FOWND) Having thoughtful depth.

suburb (SUH-buhrb) An area of homes and businesses that is near a large city.

succeed (suhk-SEED) To come after or replace someone in a position or political office.

tenant farmer (TEH-nuhnt FAR-muhr) A farmer who pays rent to work on someone else's land.

tension (TEN-shun) A state in which people, groups, or countries disagree with and feel anger toward each other.

white supremacist (WYT suh-PREH-muh-sist) Someone who believes that white people are better than those of other groups.

INDEX

PRIMARY SOURCE LIST

Page 9
Governor Ellis Arnall of Georgia. Photograph. Bettmann. Taken in Washington, D.C. October 20, 1943. From Getty Images.

Page 13
Black voters line up to cast ballots. Photograph. Bettmann. Taken in Marietta, GA. July 18, 1946. From Getty Images.

Page 25
Hamilton Holmes and Charlayne Hunter at the University of Georgia's 160th commencement ceremony. Photograph. Associated Press. Taken in Athens, GA. June 3, 1963. From AP Images.

WEBSITES

Due to the changing nature of Internet links, PowerKids Press has developed an online list of websites related to the subject of this book. This site is updated regularly. Please use this link to access the list: www.powerkidslinks.com/sog/dawwii